# Meet
# Abraham Lincoln

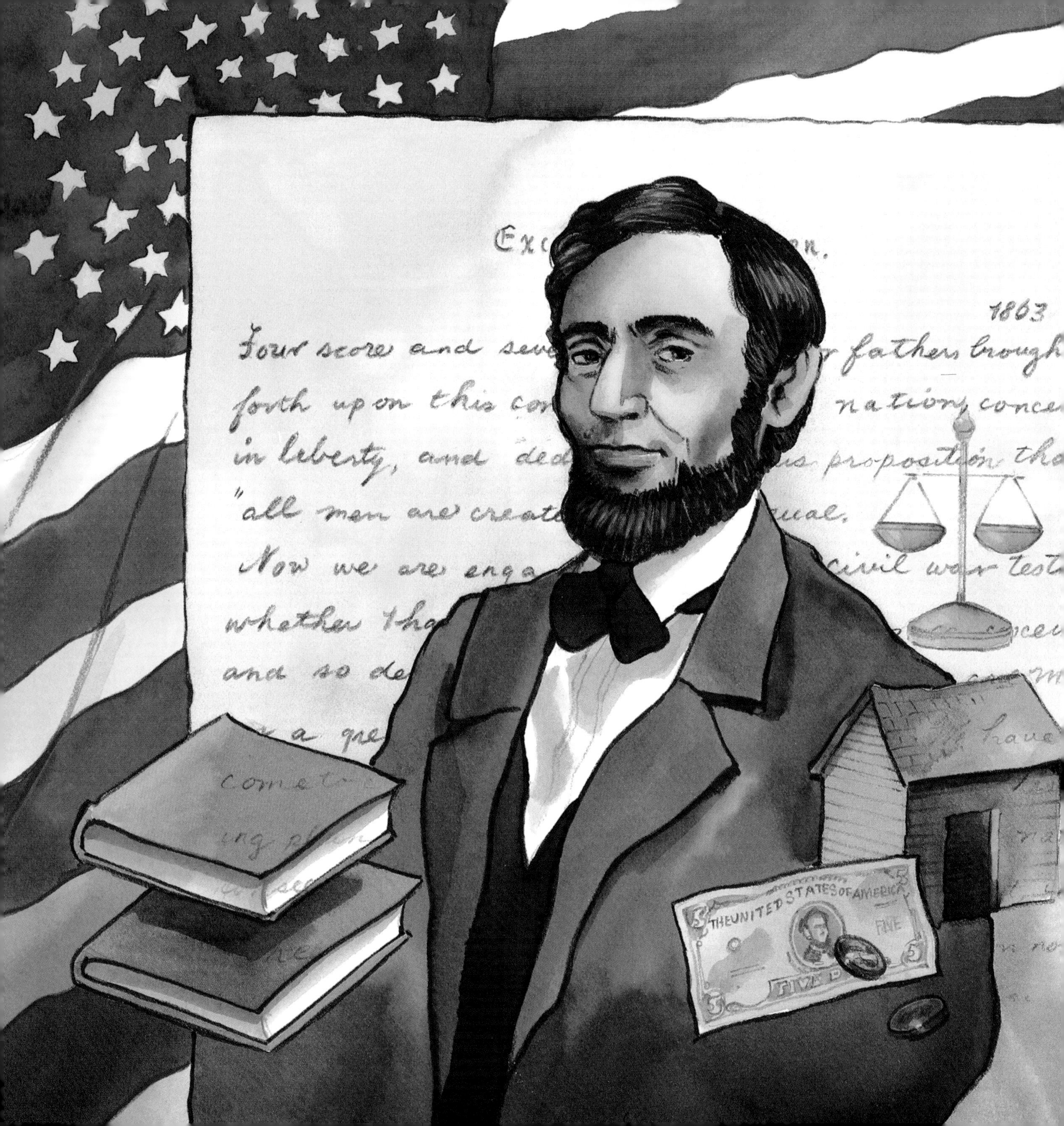
1863
THE UNITED STATES OF AMERICA
FIVE

# Meet
# Abraham Lincoln

by Patricia A. Pingry

Illustrated by Stephanie McFetridge Britt

Nashville, Tennessee

ISBN 0-8249-4132-2

Published by Ideals Children's Books
An imprint of Ideals Publications
A division of Guideposts
535 Metroplex Drive, Suite 250
Nashville, Tennessee 37211
www.idealsbooks.com

Library of Congress Cataloging-in-Publication data on file

Printed and bound in Mexico by R.R. Donnelley

Color separations by Precision Color Graphics, Franklin, Wisconsin

10 9 8 7 6 5 4 3 2 1

Designed by Eve DeGrie

*Thank you to Dorothy Twohig, Editor-in-Chief Emeritus, The Papers of
George Washington, University of Virginia, for reading this manuscript and
offering her comments.*

**For Nicholas**

Four score and seven years ago our fathers brought forth on this continent, a new nation, conceived in Liberty, and dedicated to the proposition that all men are created equal. . . .

We here highly resolve that these dead shall not have died in vain— that this nation, under God, shall have a new birth of freedom— and that government of the people, by the people, for the people, shall not perish from the earth.

—Abraham Lincoln, at Gettysburg, Pennsylvania, battlefield, 1863

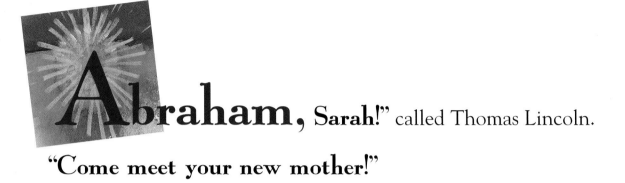

# Abraham, Sarah!" called Thomas Lincoln. "Come meet your new mother!"

Ten-year-old Abraham Lincoln looked up from the log he was splitting. He saw his father unhook the horse from the wagon as his sister, Sarah, came around the corner of the cabin. She was holding her apron that cradled freshly dug potatoes. Fall had been in the air for days and the children knew the potatoes must be dug and the woodpile stacked before the winter freeze came.

Thomas Lincoln had just arrived home from a trip to Hodgenville,

Kentucky. Abraham had been born in Hodgenville on February 12,

1809, and the Lincolns had lived there until one day in the autumn of

1816. That was the day Thomas Lincoln packed up his family and

crossed the Ohio River into the Indiana wilderness.

Life in Indiana was hard, and they struggled through the winter. In the spring, eight-year-old Abraham helped his father cut down trees and build a small cabin. When Abraham was nine, his mother, Nancy Hanks, died. Now, a year later, Abraham still missed his mother very much.

After their mother died, Abraham and Sarah went to school for a little while. But when spring came, Abraham had to quit school and help his dad with the farm work.

But today, Abraham's father was coming back home with a full wagon and a new wife. Abraham leaned his big ax against the logs and started toward the cabin.

"**Here comes Abraham**," said Thomas Lincoln. "**And here is my daughter, Sarah.**"

"**Hello, Abraham**," said the new Mrs. Lincoln, holding out her hands to the children. "**Sarah, we have the same first name. My name is Sarah Bush Johnston, and we are all going to get along just fine.**"

Sarah Bush Johnston followed the children into the cabin.

"**Oh, my,**" she said when she went inside. "**We have some cleaning to do.**"

Abraham helped Thomas unload Sarah's furniture. He helped her unpack the silver knives, spoons, and forks. Abraham had never seen such beautiful things.

He watched Sarah Bush Johnston clean the cabin and set the table, and he smelled the wonderful stew she made. She told Abraham stories about life in Kentucky. He told her about the books he had read. They became friends, and Abraham soon called her "Mama." She made him feel special.

Sometimes Abraham's father hired him out to help other settlers.

Abraham chopped down their trees, built their fences, dug their wells.

They paid his father as much as twenty-five cents a day for Abraham's help.

Abraham didn't like chopping trees or building fences or digging wells. He liked to read and he wanted to learn all that he could. Sometimes Abraham walked miles just to borrow a book. Then he walked miles to return it. At night, after his chores, he liked to read by the light of the fire.

When Abraham was nineteen, he was about six feet, four inches tall. A local merchant hired him to go to New Orleans with the merchant's son.

The boys used long poles to push a flatboat down the Ohio and Mississippi rivers. They pushed the boat twelve hundred miles.

In New Orleans, Abraham first saw slaves. He never forgot the sight of people being sold. Abraham knew that in New Orleans, slavery was allowed; it was the law. But Abraham knew that slavery was wrong, and he wondered if somebody could change that law.

In 1830, the Lincolns left Indiana and moved to Illinois. Abraham helped his father build another cabin. Then Abraham said good-bye to his family and moved to another small town in Illinois called New Salem.

Abraham found a job in a store. He liked to talk to the customers and tell them funny stories that made them laugh. To prove that he was a good sport, he even wrestled the local wrestling champ and won! Abraham made many friends in New Salem. In 1834 the little town of New Salem elected Abraham to the Illinois state legislature.

Abraham wanted to be successful and help others. He began to think that he would like to be a lawyer. He was too poor to go to college; but he read and studied the law for three years. In 1836, he passed the Illinois bar exam. Now he could practice law. Abraham became a successful lawyer who was known for his honesty. People called him "honest Abe." Abraham still told funny stories.

In 1837, he packed all his things into his saddlebags and moved to Springfield, Illinois.

Abraham soon fell in love with a beautiful young woman named Mary Todd. She was also from Kentucky but lived in Springfield with her sister. She and Abraham wanted to marry, but Mary's father thought she could find somebody more successful than Abraham. In November 1842, Mary married Abraham anyway. They had four sons.

In 1860, Abraham was asked to run for president of the United States. The southern states did not want a president who did not like slavery, but Abraham was elected anyway. On March 4, 1861, he became the sixteenth president of the United States.

When Abraham was elected president, eleven southern states decided to form their own country: the Confederate States of America. As president, Abraham would not let the United States be split in half.

When the Confederate States fired upon Fort Sumter, South Carolina, the American Civil War began.

Abraham and Mary moved their family into the White House. Their two younger sons, Willie and Tad, had a lot of fun there. The boys rode their pony on the White House lawn. Their goat slept in their beds. They ran through the hallways and into their father's cabinet meetings.

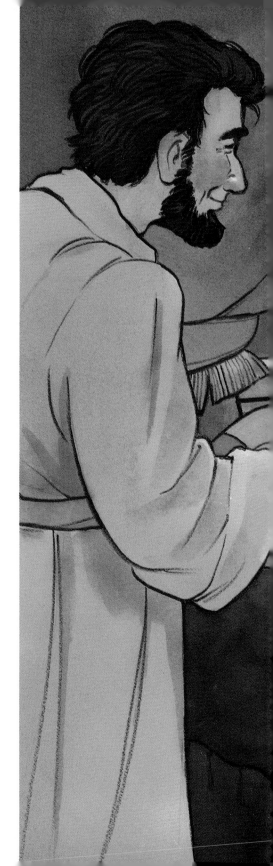

Abraham loved having his boys in the White House. He laughed at their games. They laughed at his stories.

Abraham still remembered the slaves in New Orleans. He wanted to free all slaves. In the South, slavery was the law, but Abraham wanted to change that law. On January 1, 1863, he issued the Emancipation Proclamation. Now all slaves in the United States were free.

On April 9, 1865, after five long years, the Confederate States surrendered. The Civil War was over. The United States was back together: South and North as one country.

One beautiful spring day, Abraham and Mary went for a buggy ride. Abraham told her funny stories to make her laugh. That night, they went to a play at Ford's Theatre in Washington, D.C. An actor, John Wilkes Booth, shot and killed Abraham. There would be no more funny stories.

A train took Abraham's body back home to Springfield, Illinois. Black people and white people stood together along the railroad tracks. They came to say goodbye to the president they called "Father Abraham."

To remember Abraham, we put his picture on the five-dollar bill and on the penny. To honor him, we built the Lincoln Memorial in Washington, D.C.

Abraham fought a war to keep our country one United States. He fought a war to make all Americans free. And he . . .

told many funny stories.